EXCEL MODELING BEST PRACTICES

Learn how to Structure your Workbooks.

by

Dan Goldfynn

I0504254

HOW TO READ THIS BOOK

This book is meant to be read with as little overhead as possible. Read it in the lounge, on the bed, waiting for the plane, curled up on the sofa. No preparation is required. There are no assignments, no worksheets, no quizzes, and no problems to solve.

There is a sample Excel workbook (go to https://thetechsavvymanager.com) you can download to explore the described concepts, but you can always refer to it after reading and absorbing the concepts.

Just sit down (or lie down).

Read.

Structuring Excel Models, Copyright © 2023 by Dan Goldfynn.

Printed in the United States of America

V3.0

TABLE OF CONTENTS

1. INTRODUCTION

Excel is a powerful tool. It's arguably the most widely used spreadsheet program, and the majority of the world's "models" live in some Excel workbook or the other.

I've spent many years working for companies and consultancies and have spent countless hours building Excel models. I have also wasted a good portion of my life figuring out someone else's models or explaining mine to someone else.

All this led to some simple observations when it comes to Excel modeling.

1. *A lot of people know how to use Excel* — from creating simple tables and computations

2. *Fewer people know how to use some of the easier, yet powerful Excel features* — from Pivot tables to INDEX/MATCHes

3. *Even fewer people know how to build models* — from simple lookup models to truly hairy, scary macro-riddled monstrosities that no one except the creator can understand

4. *…And even fewer* know how to structure models in a way that's easy to follow and transfer to someone else, catch errors, and update over time.

In this book, we will learn a pretty simple and straightforward method that you can use to structure most models. The models *do not* have to be complicated to take advantage of this methodology.

Just to set expectations, this book DOES NOT teach you how to build a specific model, like a revenue forecasting model or a price optimization model. But what it does is it shows a method for constructing any models in a Workbook such that it is easy to follow and manage. This is also not a book to teach you Excel basics. We don't spend time on specific formulae or how to write functions, or how to deploy vlookups or INDEX(MATCH()). What we do instead is figure out how to build a model using best practices at a structural level.

I have used this technique (and so have many others I know) effectively in a wide variety of work, including high-stress consulting and strategy projects with some of the best-known corporations in the world. I didn't come up with all of this–it's a combination of what I learned from smart people and made little improvements of my own.

This is not one of those *"let me tell you how to make a million dollars even though I can barely get by"* stories. As you read it, you might even wonder — is this it? Not fancier and cooler? The key to maintainability is *simplicity*. The greater the number of rules and structure, the harder it is to understand, train and transfer. So, the approach outlined here is a happy medium between the chaos of unstructured Workbooks and the mind-numbing bureaucracy of heavily regulated Workbooks.

2. PRE-REQUISITES

- *Microsoft Excel*. Of course. This book is all about Excel. But the good news is, the techniques outlined here have *nothing to do with Excel* for most parts — you can employ it in any spreadsheet program using native methods. The approach here is more of a concept than a proprietary feature of Excel.

- *Patience*. Like anything new, it requires some patience to learn and believe that this might work.

1.1 EXAMPLE EXCEL MODEL

- Go to https://thetechsavvymanager.com/#sem and download the template spreadsheet that you can use to look at an implementation.

- The case-sensitive password to the sheet is provided later in this book.

1.2 TERMS AND DEFINITIONS

Just so that there's no confusion. In this book —

- *Workbook*: The full Excel file

- *Worksheet*: An individual sheet within a workbook

- *Tab*: The little tab at the bottom of a Worksheet. Every Worksheet has a tab.

1.3 GUIDING PRINCIPLES

This guide, and my general philosophy to Excel modeling work, is to follow two basic guiding principles

- *Simplicity is key to explainability* — keep your organization as simple and self-explanatory as possible. It is better to use a series of simple calculations than to do the same with impressive yet complex and difficult-to-understand formulae.

- *Self-describing Worksheets beat separate documentation* — if you label all your Worksheets and drivers and variables and tables and graphs and add notes below (or above) them on intent, your work is already self-documenting and will require little other external guides and documents. You will avoid maintenance and out-of-sync nightmares.

1.4 HOW TO READ THIS BOOK

In line with my other **"Keep It Simple"** series, this book is meant to be read whichever way you want. In a hotel lounge, on a plane, on the couch, in a hair stylist waiting area, at the doctor's waiting to get your teeth drilled, in front of a computer, at the team room… anywhere.

You do not need to sit in front of a computer to read this, and you are not required to complete "lessons" at the end of each chapter.

Read it comfortably, absorbing the concepts. Once you finish, download the sample template to see how some concepts are implemented. The only section best done with the model is the Error Checks — but you can choose not to.

That's it.

1.5 WHAT THIS BOOK IS NOT

This is not an Excel for Dummies or Excel for Experts book. This book will not teach you how to use Excel or the various formulae. I do expect that you know the basics of Excel or perhaps even advanced enough to be building models. Experts in Excel might even recognize many areas where you can use "smarter ways" and more sophisticated formulae—and all that is fine, except that demonstrating "cool ways" to do things is not the objective of this book. Besides, I have always maintained *simplicity* as one of my tenets and, where possible, have usually avoided trying to be too smart.

2.   SEPARATION OF CONCERNS

What's "separation of concerns"? Originally applied to software programming, separation of concerns simply means a system can be decomposed to several constituent components with specific intent.

For example, one component is only concerned with storing data. Another component interprets the data. Another displays the output. Why do we do that? Separation ensures that so long as each component knows how to interact with the other (through a standard input/output), you can improve or replace one without affecting the other. It makes understanding a complex system easier, more manageable to maintain and manage, and to improve independently of the other.

You see the separation of concerns everywhere around you in life.

You don't need to break an entire house to install a door.

You can swap out wheels in a car without buying a new car.

You can (or should be able to) improve the user interface of your application without changing all the data access code.

While separation of concerns is very commonly enforced, either unconsciously (through design rules of individual components) or consciously (through reviews and audits), in the software and hardware worlds, it is almost completely ignored in the "Excel users'" world (except maybe in little corners of finance and management consulting).

Most Excel models you see in the real world are messy — from mildly inconvenient to horrendous hell.

Here are some common Excel model issues.

1. No table titles or explanation to what's in the workbook. *Who needs to know what it's all about?*

2. No labeling of input variables. *Let's guess the intent of everything and hope they're used where/how they are supposed to be.*

3. No discernible order to the considerable number of tabs in the workbook. *Why care for order when chaos is so easy!*

4. No order or sense to the data, calculations, graphs—all intermingled with each other. *Mix 'em up and watch the world…er, Workbook burn!*

5. Exceedingly noisy Worksheet—*why split anything across tabs when you can cram everything into one?!*

6. No unit labeling—*yes, millions, billions, hours, dollars, pounds, pesos, years… whatever.*

7. No error checks—is this model producing the right output? *Maybe. Maybe not. Could be.*

8. Mysterious split across workbooks. Where some parts of the model are in one, and the rest are in the other, with no explanation of how they're connected.

9. Complexity for complexity's sake—*why make it easy when you can make it hard?*

10. No source attributions or completely massaged data—*where did this data come from? Client? Aliens? Imagination? Who knows! Who cares?*

We will use the concept of separation of concerns in this guide and show how you can structure your work in a simple and intuitive way that benefits you, your team, and whoever gets to live with your work long after you're gone (from the building, of course).

3.   REAL-WORLD INSTANCES

There is always a risk with books like these that the author may be making up a make-believe world where everything is perfect, pedantic, and inspirationally awesome, but with little to no practical application. It's like a book that says, "how to make a million dollars writing books," by an author who's selling two $2.99 books per week.

Fear not, brave *spreadsheeters*, the techniques outlined in this book have been tried and tested many times, over years, across companies and teams, and used not just by me but also by many others who use similar techniques.

Here are five real-world problems that were solved using Excel models built using the techniques outlined in this book and eventually handed over to others. In no order:

- *Whether to build a new company owned Data Center or move to a Public Cloud* (if you don't know what the heck I'm talking about, I think it's time to get a little tech savvy)—the model split the cost of building (facilities, operations, labor, infrastructure, hardware, software) and compared the use case with moving to one of four major Public Clouds using their licensing costs.

- *Whether to change the shift resourcing in a Call Center to better optimize for traffic and customer experience*—the model created a series of "Erlang-C" computations based on various input variables to create a shift heatmap

- *Whether to sell a specific type of precious metal or keep hedging against market fluctuations*—the model created a multi-year scenario with various hypothetical drivers of the impact to the business if they held on to the metal vs. conducting a series of sell and buys based on usage cycles

- *Whether to change the mix of vendors supplying products*—the model looked at the products and their margins over years, along with various incentives offered by and for the vendor, across vendors, to decide whether a supplier list had to be pruned and what such pruning would lead to in terms of improved incentives.

- *Whether the business unit was making a profit or a loss* – the model looked at the unit's sales and cost figures, adjusted for all kinds of internal transfer costs and mismanaged finances, to work out whether the unit was making profits or losses in the last few years

4. DANGERS OF BAD MODELS

No, we're not talking about your difficult life with scantily clad models with bad attitude, but the ramifications of using bad Excel (or any Spreadsheet) models.

- *Strained credibility*—this is the biggest danger, and especially serious in certain types of professions where you are expected to go up and explain an outcome to senior executives. Even minor mistakes can sometimes throw off an entire presentation (*how can I believe the rest of your analysis?*) and cause embarrassment (or worse) to you and your manager(s)

- *Frustrated clients and teams*—You will either deal with frustration during model transfer, or worse, the client keeps coming back after the transfer because they're struggling with it. It's a problem neither of you want.

- *Serious implications*—It is not uncommon for a model mistake to get through the reviews and cross checks (we sometimes call it "*bullshit test*" to see if some numbers simply intuitively make no sense. Is it possible that a young company has 400 billion $ in sales? Guess not), but then when the output starts getting used and decisions are made on its basis, even simple mistakes can lead to serious consequences and public embarrassment.

- *Misrepresentation or Lost in Translation*—When you hand over the model to someone and it's a mess, it often leads to them misunderstanding intent or mishandling the content. This will sometimes lead to a branding problem—where you're attached to the model even though someone else misunderstood it.

As I mentioned at the beginning of this book, Excel models are pervasive and used in most enterprises and universities. The world is awash with horrible spreadsheets, and hopefully you will be one of those few who does not perpetuate this horror!

5.   ANATOMY OF A MODEL

Note: The case-sensitive password for the sample Excel workbook available on https://thetechsavvymanager.com/ is SEMTMPL (go to the book page and look for bonus)

Any model has three principal components, each with its own "concern." Let's start with that.

- Input — what feeds the model

- Calculation — what you calculate

- Output — results and what you show

You could technically just compose your Workbook in these three parts. That doesn't mean you know the best ways to organize those components, but at least you're one step better than a single-Worksheet mess.

Let us go a level deeper into this structure and introduce an extra section (index)

5.1 GENERAL WORKBOOK STRUCTURE

```
-  Index (INDEX)

   -   Introduction

   -   Index Jump and Error Summary

   -   Documentation

-  Input (INPUT)

   -   Data

   -   Variables/Assumptions

   -   Drivers

-  Calculations (CALC)

   -   Intermediate

   -   Final

-  Output (OUTPUT)

   -   Tables
```

- Graphs

- Summaries

- Backup and Appendix

Now, there is such a thing as over-engineering. In some cases, even the split above may be too much, so you must exercise discretion and not force a rigid structure down your (or anyone else's) throat if it doesn't warrant it. Having said that, most meaningfully complex models can benefit greatly from the above.

Should each sub-bullet be on a separate Worksheet?

The short answer is "yes" if there's a lot of data and variables. "No" if it's relatively short. I prefer at least one tab per section, though many large models will need to split some of the sub-bullets in multiple sections, for example, *data*.

Next, let's look at how to organize a workbook along the above sections before we dive into each.

5.2 STRUCTURING A WORKBOOK

We will do three things as part of structuring a workbook, using the sections outlined before.

1. Group each top level and its sub-levels into a tab group

2. Separate each tab group with a divider tab labeled with the top level

3. Color each tab group with a separate color

Each of those tabs should have their sub-sections, like below (they are hidden in the screenshot)

Now, on each worksheet, set up an "Error Check" cell pair on the top-left. For now, in c2, set up conditional formatting so that if c2 = 0, then it's light green, and if it is not equal (<>) to 0, then red. We'll talk about how to use that later in this guide.

A	B	C	D	
	Pulls relevant data from raw data and			
	CHECK	0		
	Computed Columns added			
	Pay Rank: to determine pay position of employe			
	Wage Group: Assign 1, 2, or 3 based on Pay sc			
	Emp #	Satisfaction Sco	Last Evaluatic	Nu
	E8_4	0.38	0.53	
	E20 5	0.8	0.86	

With that, your workbook is now structured! That wasn't so hard. Now let's dive into each section and what to do there.

6. MANAGING SECTIONS

In this section, we will go through every one of the structuring sections. We will talk about usage, hygiene, tips, and watchouts. This is a long chapter, so take it easy and go one by one.

First, here's a simple visual of the flow of your model construction.

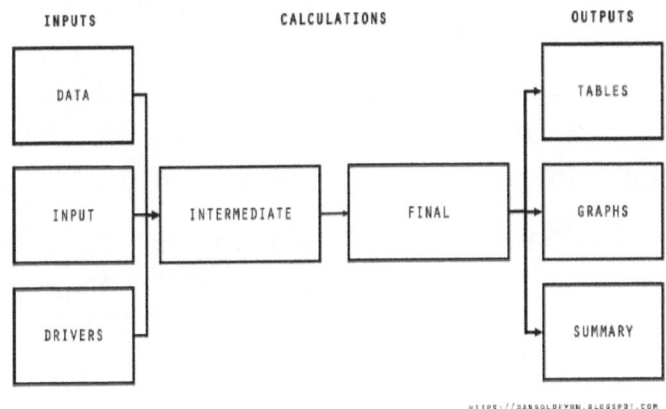

If you are so inclined, this may also be the time to get the sample Excel template from the site https://thetechsavvymanager.com (go to the specific book area) to get an idea of some of the tactics below. You can alternatively just relax on your couch and just read all this and absorb the ideas, and then look at the spreadsheet.

6.1 DATA

Data is self-explanatory. These tabs hold data. For example, employees and their salary, companies and their margins, vendors, and their product details, and so on. You can divide data into additional sections as needed. and massaged/formatted data (cleaned up, columns added, reformatted to make it more usable)

7. RAW DATA

This is raw data as given by the client/source. Oftentimes, people forget to include the raw data in the final model. They massage and format it nicely and then start from there. It is always good to keep the original data as-is for many reasons

- *For traceability/auditability and integrity*—so that if the model is called to question, then you have the original, unformatted data as given to you

- *For client comfort*—Many people who provide data want to see it in the format they gave it to you in, or they will not "recognize" it, so it's also in your best interest to keep the original, no matter how ugly, as-is and then use other means to clean it up.

- *For independent error checks*—Raw data is also a great source for independent error checks to ensure you did not mess with it while copying/transferring it elsewhere.

The exception for not keeping raw data is when it is so huge that it is impractical to keep in the model—in such cases, you would need to build a subset, clearly mention the source in your Workbook, and always provide the raw with the model when you transfer your work.

8.   CLEANSED DATA

Cleansed data is where you "massage" the raw data and keep it in a form that's easier to build computations off. Cleansed data can also have some basic new columns (like binary `true` or `false`, `1`, `0's`, simple computations, or unit conversions) that help model building. Depending on the Workbook size and raw data format, cleansed data can be cell references to the raw data or cut paste and modified. Once you have your cleansed data, your models should ONLY refer to it and not to raw data. To be clear, cleansed data may be spread in more than one tab depending on the size and intent of the data.

8.1 ASSUMPTIONS AND DRIVERS

All models have two broad types of input apart from data. Let's look at what they are and what goes in them. Depending on how many you have, you may split assumptions and drivers to separate tabs or keep them in the same with appropriate headings.

9.   ASSUMPTIONS/INPUTS

Most models come with a set of assumptions or static inputs that feed into them. Here's a simple list of types of assumptions.

```
Average conversion $ to GBP

Industry benchmark profits for sector

Peak cost per pound of X

Average number of people per family per major region

Median pay

Growth rate for next 5 years
```

It's always good practice to list assumptions in a clear table with a description of the variable and the unit (don't forget the unit!). The screenshot below demonstrates the idea.

Key Assumptions and Input

Variable	Value		Unit	Notes
Above Market Threshold (Wage Group 1)	$	120	'000 USD	Based on HR Benchmark 2019
Below Market Threshold (Wage Group 3)	$	65	'000 USD	Based on Gartner report 2019

10. DRIVERS

The output of any model is "driven" by a set of considerations. Drivers are usually very important, whether in financial valuations, M&A computations, profit projections, sales forecasts and so on. Sometimes it may be hard to distinguish between an input and a driver—the simplest way to think about it is *"input is what stays constant in the lifecycle of your model, driver is what you change to impact the outcome."*

Let's look at some examples of drivers. A model can have more than one driver—in fact, it's common for a model to have multiple drivers that you change to come up with various scenarios.

- *Growth YoY*—where you're changing the annual growth projection to see implications for some sort of overall revenue or profit goal

- *Advertising Expense as % of Marketing Cost*—where you're modeling to see what happens as expenses go up or down

- *$/unit projection*—where you're seeing what happens to your margins if unit costs go up/down

You would set up a driver table just like the Input/Assumptions table. The key difference, to re-iterate, is that you will be changing the driver to come up with various scenarios where inputs/assumptions stay constant.

Drivers

Variable	Wage Group	Option 1	Option 2	Option 3
Decreases to Wage Group	1	3%	10%	15%
Increases to Wage Group	3	6%	8%	20%

10.1 CALCULATIONS ("CALC")

This is where the magic happens. CALC is the heart of your Workbook. In these tabs, which may be more than one, you break the model into one or more progressive components to arrive at your answers. All calculations don't have to happen in a single tab as it may get complicated and messy. Sometimes, it helps to create progressive layers of calculations, where the first tab could be a large table with tons of calculations, the next is a shorter version that summarizes/indexes parts, and the final is the "final list of outputs." Such an approach reduces excessive complexity packed into any single model portion and makes it much easier to debug and catch errors.

The way you can structure it is by using two groups of tabs (a) *Intermediate* — where you're still working through various values and (b) *Final* — which takes values from intermediate to get to the final outputs.

CALC is also where commenting, clear labeling, and error checks are critical. Here are some tips for this section.

1. *Enforce no hard-coded or manual input rule* — nothing in this sheet must be a manual input. Everything is either referenced from *Inputs* or *Drivers* or is a calculation.

2. *Follow a solution order* — go left to right or top to bottom for your various solution sections

3. *Eschew complex formulae in favor of breaking it down to progressive steps* — for example, instead of a column with multiple nested IFs, you are better off breaking each into a column with switches

(Yes/Nos or 1/0's) and then building the next using the previous as input

4. *Follow a simple and consistent cell coloring rule*—what I have seen work effectively is following some basic rules

   - Light gray on all cells that are computed (i.e. there's a formula in there)—this makes it easy to quickly convey the idea that NOTHING on this sheet is changed manually

   - Light yellow if you are making a direct reference to an input or a drive (so the reader knows how you're using it in the sheet)

   - Light Orange to indicate that this is a manual input (e.g., drivers)

Yellow	Referenced cells
Gray	Computed/Calculated cells
Blue	Headers and Labels
Orange	Manual Input

5. *Build copious error checks*—since CALC sheets are the heart of your models, as many sensible error checks you can build here, the better. The integrity of your model can be preserved to a great extent with some robust error checking. We will cover this in greater detail in a dedicated chapter.

10.2 OUTPUT TABLES

OUTPUT is where you begin to assemble your final product that is getting ready to consume—as snippets in emails, in PowerPoint presentations, Memos, straight-forward Excels, web pages—whatever it is. The OUTPUT should have the final set of value(s) that answers whatever the objective of the model.

There are really two principal ways to depict an output, and let's look at both.

11. TABLES

This is where you depict the answers in a simple Excel table. It is always a good practice to build your Output tables instead of graphing them directly, because a table will let you further filter, sort, pull sub-sets, and so on and can, in many instances, be simple to consume.

Some tips on building output tables

1. If relevant, reference the drivers and the final output values, coloring the references and output values — this makes it easy to see what drove what results.

2. Build a comprehensive table and then build progressive tables that are a subset if needed (e.g., a full table of the range of outputs, summaries, short-lists, ranked tables) by referencing the full table.

3. Do NOT use any hardcoded values anywhere in OUTPUT. All our OUTPUT should be computed or referenced from CALC and INPUT (only to reference).

4. Avoid computing new model outputs within OUTPUT. This tab should only be pulling results and assembling values.

12. DISPLAY

This is where you either build charts for visual displays or text sentences (e.g., "The margin for the products rose by $x for scenario Y") for copy-paste in emails or periodic reporting updates. Displays are usually built off chart tables and should follow similar rules.

It is always a good idea to have displays as a tab on their own so that the graphics are laid out with their titles in a meaningful order. The other reason to have a DISPLAY separately is that you can treat is an executive dashboard with all visual necessary messaging in a single place.

13. DOCUMENTATION

There are many ways you can document a model. Here are three popular methods—I favor the simpler, second method, but I have seen the first employed as well.

1. *With a flow diagram*—where you depict the flow of the model through a diagram that shows the key drivers and major computational algorithms that drive the results. Flow diagrams are reasonably easy to follow but *they are devilishly hard to maintain.* Every time you make any modifications, it's almost guaranteed that you will not go back to change major flow diagrams. Implementing a flow diagram may work if you've done everything else, locked your model down, no more changes, and then you document the flow and hand the Workbook over.

2. *In simple English*—just describe the model in plain English. This is usually the best method, it's easy to follow if you structure your Workbook, and it's easy to maintain if there are changes. The idea is that your structuring should already self-describe the model, and the text gives additional context and clarity. The text method does NOT require that you describe every calculation in gory detail, but that you only point out key concepts behind the model and highlight the major algorithmic approaches to the solution. The principle behind this thinking is that someone trying to use such a model is probably capable of proceeding from thoughtful instructions rather than needing to be told how to do every single calculation.

3. *Detailed breakdown of the model*—with full pseudocode and all drivers documented separately. Sounds good. Terrible idea.

14. ERROR CHECKS

Note: The case-sensitive password for the sample Excel workbook available on https://thetechsavvymanager.com.com/ is SEMTMPL (go to the book page and look for bonus)

This is an important section and often the most ignored in modeling spreadsheets. How do you minimize the chance that your model has errors? Perhaps this comes as a surprise to you, or perhaps not, but I would bet that vast majority of Excel Workbooks in the world have no error checks built into them—none. Not even basic checks. That is because most of us never learned about robust error checks when we were initiated into Excel modeling.

There are many horror stories of math being off my orders of magnitude and presenters being caught by embarrassing mistakes that could have otherwise been caught by basic error checks. (*Your company grew by 10400% last year, really?*)

We will learn some simple error check techniques in guide—it's nothing fancy, but it is effective. The principle of error checks across a Workbook follows a very simple approach.

At a Workbook Level:

```
Error Check = SUM(of all Worksheet-level error check cells)

If (Error Check > 0) Then (There is an Error)
```

At a Worksheet level

```
Error Check = SUM(of all error check cells within the sheet)

If (Error Check > 0) Then (There is an Error)
```

That's all there is to it. The Workbook level checks should show up in the Index sheet of the Workbook—something like this:

14.1 WORKBOOK LEVEL ERROR CHECK AND INDEX

Here are some implementation tips

	Description	Error Check
1	Formatted Data	Raw data from Source: Kaggle.com HR Data for Analytics Public Domain Dataset	0
2	Variables	Pulls relevant data from raw data and adds additional classification columns based on input var	0
3	Drivers	Wage Adjustment Scenarios	0
4	Intermediate Ca	Compute Wage Expense by Department by Wage Group	0
5	Final Calculatio	Compute Savings and Expenses Per Strategic Option	0
6	Output Tables	Compute Final Net Benefits by Strategic Option	0
7	Graphs	Executive Graphs	0

1. *Build a line for every Worksheet* — including inputs and display

2. *Have a final sum-up so you can see it as soon as you get to the sheet.* If it's red (based on conditional formatting where `if (>0) then color(red)`)

3. *You can use the tab index for both Table of Contents purpose AND error check* — it's all in one.

4. You can build an *"error-check error check"* by summing all independent error check cells across the entire Workbook as an ultimate error cross-check!

5. It's good practice to pull the Worksheet description from it rather than hardcoding it in the table. For example, in the image above, the description is a reference cell to each Worksheet. This ensures that each Worksheet is self-contained and described.

14.2 WORKSHEET LEVEL ERROR CHECK

The real check is at this level. Let's first go through the guiding principles of *what* makes sense as an error check and what this is all about.

1. An error check is an *independent computation,* or a cross-check of a set of values that must result in a match

2. A Worksheet can have several error checks. Make your life easy by following the same principle for all error checks so that they are visually obvious at first look (i.e., make them all bordered two-cells, with conditionally formatted to red for >0 and green for =0)

At this point, I would strongly suggest you go get the Example Excel Template and study a few tabs to understand the concept. Here is a simple explanation.

Let's first take a simple data table in DATA, and you built a model in CALC that computes the total importance for each category. It would be this:

Cat/Imp	A	B
X	10	15
Y	5	10
Z	20	25

Cat	Importance
X	25
Y	15
Z	45

Error Check	

Now the error check on this table would be

`EC = SUM(of CALC Importance) — SUM(of all A and B cells in DATA)`

As you can see, the error check comes to a value match through an independent means. If your work is correct, then EC = 0. If you introduced an error in CALC or added some hard-coded numbers, EC will instantly flip to <> 0.

The example spreadsheet shows you several such error checks from DATA and is worth studying. Creating error checks can significantly cut the introduction of errors in the Workbook. It may not eliminate everything, and if you overdo it, you risk building useless and sometimes erroneous error checks; so be judicious. If the error check is not comprised of **independent calculations**, *it is not an error check.*

14.3 TYPES OF ERROR CHECKS

There are two major types of checks. One is an independent cross-check (the one shown above). The other is a bound or hard-coded *"known fact"* check. Let's talk about the second one a little more.

Consider the variables in INPUT or the drivers in DRIVERS. They are not computed values and there's nothing to compare them against — what do you do then?

Do you abandon error checks?

Do you put empty cells with '0' values

Do you ignore the sheet for any error check?

No.

You can still build error checks, but you use a *known facts* method. What this means is you can use bounds, totals, ranges, averages and other mathematical constructs to ensure that the values contained fall within that.

For example, if you use a growth projection model and you use five scenarios (5%, 10%, ...) then your independent check can check if

```
ANY of the values > 20% (i.e. your model should not have a scenario where growth
is projected < 20%)
```

```
ANY of the values <1%
```

```
SUM of all percentages <50%
```

```
Profit < $1B
```

These checks ensure that, for example, someone does not accidentally enter ridiculous growth rates. You just need to be careful that the cross-checks are based on numbers you know to be reasonable for the model.

This is just an example: there are many other ways you can enter bounds for the values, and the intention is to ensure you do not have unreasonable entries.

15. NOTES ON SAMPLE EXCEL MODEL

Get the Sample Excel model first before you begin this section. This demonstrates many of the concepts of this book using a simple model. The file is self-explanatory (except for the caveats and tips found here), and you should start from Index and progress to the right.

15.1 OBSERVATIONS AND CAVEATS

- You will notice that the Index section is just one Worksheet rather than 3 tabs. This demonstrates that you don't always have to have everything in separate tabs when it makes sense, so long as you have the necessary content in a not-busy fashion.

- There are clever ways to pull descriptions and error check values using the INDIRECT() formula, but as I have said before—sometimes simplicity is key.

- The Worksheet error checks are not exhaustive—a few have been shown to demonstrate how it can be done. Go and hard-code change numbers in many of the tables, and you will see an instant ripple of error from the Worksheet to the Index

- Yes, you absolutely can combine sparse Worksheets—for example, the Output Table and Display could theoretically be a single Worksheet. The separation of Worksheets *within a section* makes sense when one starts getting busy and harder to follow

- In CALC/Intermediate, it is possible to build the tables using Excel pivots. The benefit of building with SUMIFS is that if you refresh or make changes to your source data and inputs, SUMIF/INDEX/MATCH formulae change immediately and cascade through. The challenge with pivots is that it does not refresh unless you do so, and this is sometimes the source of errors. But this is a minor issue—in some cases, the pivot is the right thing to do

- Adding *Notes* in the Worksheets is a subtle way for anyone to catch any caveats in your model, special assumptions, and so on.

- In Formatted Worksheet, you will see two computed columns that pull from the Drivers tab. Now you might take a puritanical approach and say *"Never pull values from something to the right,"* and you would be right. But that might mean reproducing the entire Formatted table again in CALC just to introduce those columns—sometimes it's not worth it.

- The coloring scheme of cells is an individual preference. Don't hate me for mine! Some keep it simple (to just computed and manual), and some add even more layers (based on formulae). It is better not to overcomplicate.

- There is no explicit documentation page. This is because, in this case, the objective and the approach are straightforward and do not require copious documentation. Complex multi-stage models can benefit from some simple documentation.

16. WORKBOOK INDEPENDENCE

Sometimes, people create workbooks that link to something else or embed an external object. When you're working on your own machine, everything works. But when you send it out or transfer it to someone else, all hell breaks loose. The references no longer link, the model breaks, and the VP is hopping mad and breaking things.

An important tenet of transferable models is that the workbook is independent. But sometimes you hit challenges – for example, when the external data is too large to be included in the workbook or cannot be included as-is for other considerations (say the client doesn't want you to)

So, what do you do?

There's one broad approach that works well.

1. In Source, include the distilled or filtered sub-set your model draws from — this is the most important part. Don't build your CALC by referring to the larger source data

2. In the notes section, mention the full source and location.

The critical step here is (1), and it requires some thought. What you want to do is take the full dataset, apply filters and other extractions to get the bare minimum of what needs to drive your model, and use that as source data. You can apply this principle in 90% of the cases. There will always be exceptions why you might not be able to do this, in which case, you can do the following:

Treat your model as not a file but a folder. Then, the folder might look like this:

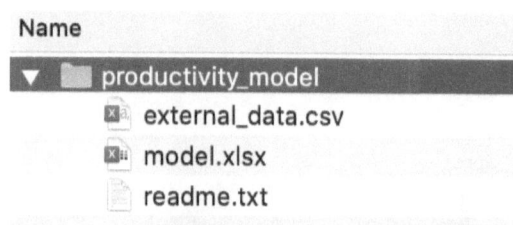

The external data is a CSV (or XLSX or anything else) is in the same folder. Use the readme.txt to explain the external data, or include it in your model readme's. When you transfer the model, transfer the entire folder.

If the external data is a web source and for whatever reason you cannot have it locally, then the only thing you can (and must) do is clearly list the source in your Workbook.

Remember, the second approach works even if you use sub-set data. The folder can contain the full original source, but the *Workbook itself is independent* and will work on its own. A client who receives a model that just… works is a happy client. Follow the simple rule: before you transfer, send it to a colleague, ask them to open the file and see if it works.

Excel has tools to identify and fix broken linkages. It's not the subject of this book but know that it's possible.

17. OBLIGATORY TOP 10

Here's a summary sheet for your convenience.

1. Any model contains `Input`, `Calculations`, and an `Output`

2. Error checks are integral to the quality of the Workbook

3. Error checks must always match independent calculations

4. Your model should be self-describing

5. Cell coloring makes it easy to interpret and understand tables

6. Simplicity strengthens *explainability*

7. Describe your notes in simple English

8. Do not over-engineer when there is no need to

9. Flow diagrams may be nice to describe the model but are incredibly hard to maintain

10. Rules are there to help but flexibility in their application is key

18. CONCLUSION

It is easy to pooh good modeling practices, but the value of doing it right cannot be underestimated. Often, the credibility of an analyst or a modeler rest on their output—and if those that you are presenting to (or producing for) catch errors in your work or have a challenging time understanding your approach, you make your life that much harder.

The rules described here are simple, and you can employ them judiciously and train others to do the same, and once you do it a few times it becomes second nature.

I hope you learned something useful, and I wish you the best in your endeavors!

END

THANK YOU

CONTINUE TO LEARN!

EASY-TO-READ BOOK SERIES

Find all at: https://thetechsavvymanager.com

The Tech Savvy Manager

Structured Excel Models

Workbook for Amazon Behavioral Interviews